I0148754

L. Herr

Forest Part Training and Breeding Farm

L. Herr

Forest Part Training and Breeding Farm

ISBN/EAN: 9783337226268

Printed in Europe, USA, Canada, Australia, Japan

Cover: Foto ©Lupo / pixelio.de

More available books at **www.hansebooks.com**

FOREST PARK

RAINING AND BREEDING FARM,

LEXINGTON, KENTUCKY.

L. HERR, PROPRIETOR.

TROTTING STALLIONS FOR SERVICE THE SEASON OF 1884.

MAMBRINO PATCHEN,
TO INSURE $100.

ARNOLD,
$50.

SIR WALTER,
$70.

MAMBRINO ABDALLAH,
$25.

LEXINGTON, KY.:
TRANSYLVANIA PRINTING COMPANY.
1884.

At Forest Park Training and Breeding Farm.

STALLIONS FOR PUBLIC SERVICE, SEASON OF 1884,

MAMBRINO PATCHEN.

Full Brother to Lady Thorn 2:18¼,

16 hands high.

By Mambrino Chief.

By Mambrino Paymaster.

By Mambrino.

By Imported Messenger.

1st dam Lady Thorn's dam by Gano, by American Eclipse, who was by Duroc and out of Miller's Damsel.

by Imp. Messenger. Gano's dam

Betsey Richards, by Sir Archey, by Imp. Diomed.

2d dam by a son of Sir William, by Sir William, who was by Sir Archey and out of Bellona, by Bellair, by Imp. Medley.

MAMBRINO PATCHEN.

TO INSURE, $100.

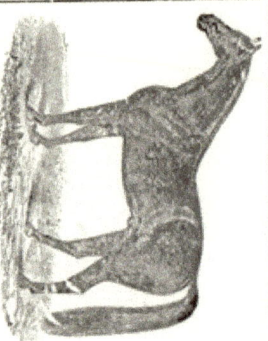

Chestnut, 16 hands high, public record 2:25½, by Aberdeen, by Hambletonian, dam by Edward Everett; 2d dam by Long Island Black Hawk; 3d dam by Exton Eclipse.

SIR WALTER.

TO INSURE, $70.

ARNOLD,

TO INSURE, $50.

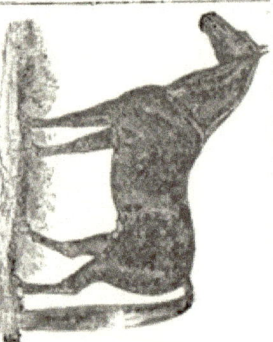

ARNOLD.

By Goldsmith's Abdallah.

By Volunteer (out of Martha, by Abdallah).

By Rysdyk's Hambletonian.

ARNOLD's dam the dam of Hambrino Belle, 2:23½, by Mambrino Chief, sire of Lady Thorn and Mambrino Patchen.

2d dam by Terror; 3d dam by Double Head; 4th dam by American Eclipse.

MAMBRINO ABDALLAH.

By Mambrino Patchen, dam a double Abdallah mare.

TO INSURE, $25.

LEXINGTON, KENTUCKY,

L. HERR, Proprietor.

MARES KEPT ON GRASS AND REGULARLY ATTENDED TO HORSES AT $5 00 PER MONTH.

Mares received and delivered at any of the Lexington, Ky., Depots free of charge.

MY VIEWS ON DEALING WITH THE PUBLIC AND SOME OTHER INTERESTING REMARKS IN RELATION TO BUSINESS.

——o——

In presenting my annual catalogue for the season of 1884 to the public, I deem it necessary to make an explanation and give my reasons for presenting it in a form different in some respects from that adopted by some of the leading breeding farms. In compiling this catalogue I have endeavored to make the pedigrees as brief as possible, and have not extended the pedigrees farther than just enough to show the desirable strains of blood contained in each animal, and have been influenced more by a desire to present the facts in as brief form as the pedigrees will admit, than by a wish to spread them and make them appear *big on paper*. I much prefer one or two good crosses close up on the dam and sire's side of the animal catalogued, even though the pedigree appears short, than to have three or four pages devoted to the bringing to notice of all the great, great, great, great grand sires, grandams, cousins, uncles and aunts, tracing back almost to the identical progenitor of the race that found refuge in the Ark. To new beginners who are not familiar with what strains of blood have produced trotters, and are fashionable and to be desired in a pedigree, these long, drawn out pedigrees are often misleading, and in purchasing an animal whose pedigree has been through *the lengthening process* they flatter themselves upon having secured a prize because the pedigree is long, and with a sense of great pride this *ancestral panorama* occupying several pages of an ordinary sized catalogue, is displayed before the wondering eyes of their uninformed neighbors and who are expected to patronize the horse should he have been bought for stud purposes. Any new beginner who is not familiar with the speed producing crosses, and who purchases one of these *long pedigreed articles* attached to three or four pages, of g, g, g, g, grand relations will, I fear, be sadly disappointed when he flatters himself that his long pedigreed stallion will command patronage from his neighbors, because, after giving the genealogy of about forty worthless generations, he traces back in his pedigree to this or that illustrious ancestor.

There is not a State or community in the Union (where it would pay to stand a horse), but what is reached by one or more of the reliable newspapers devoted to the interest of stock raising, and the people each year are becoming better informed as to which are popular and speed-producing elements in a pedigree, and their credulity can not be imposed upon by a long string of worthless crosses that amount to nothing and which are only calculated to mislead the few uninformed. One good sire and dam, positively known as possessing individual merit, are worth more in a pedigree to me than four or five pages of a catalogue filled with the names of distant ancestors, and laboring under this belief has prompted me to refrain from extending the pedigrees in this catalogue to any very great extent, merely for the sake of making them look *big.*

I don't wish to impose upon or bore intelligent men with the repetition of a long roll of names that really amount to nothing, but have endeavored to present the breeding of the stock I offer for sale in as brief and concise a form as possible. Almost any pedigree, with the assistance of the valuable stud books can be extended and drawn out until it is made to assume "Jumbo-ic" proportions, and where it becomes necessary to get one up in this style, for the sake of making up for the deficiency in close up and good crosses, the party purchasing generally find they have an elephant on hand that is hard to dispose of.

As will be seen upon an examination of this pamphlet, I omit all foot notes, merely giving the color, age, records, and pedigrees of each animal so far as known and believed to be correct. The addition of foot notes, giving description, promise of speed, disposition, &c., may be regarded by some as one of the most essential things in a catalogue, and while I admit they are sometimes useful, in giving information to parties who contemplate purchasing a colt, still I think there is a better and more satisfactory way for the prospective buyer to get all the information he wants in regard to the animal he wishes to purchase, and that is for him to "come and see for himself."

Another reason why I omit foot notes is this: Take, for instance, the catalogue of almost any breeding establishment embracing from fifty to hundreds of head of stallions, mares and colts, and in scarcely any of the foot notes will you find a single word detrimental to the sale of the above animal, but each and every one possesses, in a remarkable degree, some desirable quality, is the "best gaited," the "most stylish," "very promising," "good bone," "sure to make a trotter," and such expressions and many more, make up the tone of foot notes. Now any man who is familiar with the business of conducting a breeding establishment knows from experience that where a whole stud of horses of a hundred head, or even a less number, are represented in the above terms, as is generally the case, that such cannot be a true statement of the facts, for out of so great a number there are always some that are not worthy of the mention made of them, still each and every one, are said, have one or more desirable qualities to commend it to buyers. Recognizing the fact that foot notes, as they are now generally used, are so little to be relied upon as giving a true description of the animal offered for sale, and as it appears to be "the style" to extol only the good qualities and omit the bad, I prefer to "drop out of style" and omit foot notes altogether from this catalogue, and, as I said above. *Let the buyer come and see for himself.* If any one desires to purchase, and, upon examination of this catalogue, should find anything whose breeding suits them, they can get a close description of same by letter, giving price and all information pertaining to the animal, and should they wish to purchase without seeing the animal they can do so with the assurance that it will come fully up to the description in every particular; but I much prefer that parties who want to buy, should come and make a personal examination of my stock, or when not convenient for them to do so, I would suggest that they commission some friend, upon whose judgement they can rely, to come and select for them, which would be more satisfactory both to the purchaser and myself. I am at all times pleased to exhibit my stock to visitors (whether they desire to purchase or not), and thereby give men an opportunity to judge for themselves, and I am sure they will find that the stock corresponds with the prices; not all pedigree and no horse or mare with it.

I never have, and never will, pay any correspondent of a newspaper, magazine, or monthly, to write a complimentary notice of my stock and breeding establishment (although I have had many applicants). When I wish to advertise my business, I do so in a legitimate manner, and in such a way that the public can see it is an advertisement for which I pay, and I do not resort to the subterfuge of displaying my stock and business to the public by means of complimentary articles written for the press by some traveling correspondent, whose favorable mention is simply a matter of *dollars and cents*, and the more *dollars and cents* employed, in nine cases out of ten, the more the picture is over-drawn, and the public imposed upon and made to believe that such and such a man's stock are far superior to all others, when if the truth were known and the small matter of *dollars and cents* not brought to bear on the case, there are other establishments containing just as good, and in many instances a better stud of trotters than the ones so favorably commented upon, but whose proprietors having incurred the displeasure and ill will of some of these *Traveling Authorities* by a refusal to pay them *to "write up the place"* are made the recipient of their dirty slurs, and they scarcely ever let an opportunity pass in which to give him a *dab.* I presume it requires considerable time for them to recover from the disappointment in failing to get "*the job of writing up your place,*" and from the little conscience displayed by some of them. I can't understand why it requires so much time to obliterate their hard feelings (as only gen- tlemen of character and principle are supposed to never forget an affront), I suppose they experience such a keen sense of chagrin and mortification, when after intimating that *a few dollars* would be *a rather strong incen- tive to work on,* the proprietor having *tumbled to their racket,* quietly informs them that he does not pay to have his place advertised in any but

the legitimate manner of so many words to the inch and at regular adver-
tising rates.

Now I have, from time to time, been the recipient of many kindly no-
tices in the leading newspapers of the country, and for which I feel highly
complimented and thank my friends, the editors and correspondents, and
am sincere in my appreciation of their kindness, and know that friendly
motives prompted them, as the articles were unsolicited and not a mere matter of dollars and cents, but were written voluntarily and through true
friendship.

From the above, it will be seen that I DON'T PAY WRITERS FOR BLOWING
AND MISREPRESENTING MY STOCK IN PRINT, and am not, as some breeders,
fearful that when the stock are led out for the inspection of visitors, some one
should say, *they look better on paper* than on the ground, which, I imag-
ine, would cause the owner to feel rather cheap and necessitate a considerable effort on his part to find plausible excuses for the stock not appearing
as represented.

Another point which I desire to call attention to in this card is this:
As is well known to all proprietors of stock farms, gentlemen of means,
who desire to purchase, are frequently accompanied by a so-called friend, or
judge of horse flesh, and feeling that they are not competent to judge for
themselves, rely principally upon what this pretended friend and expert may
advise in regard to making a purchase, and if he should say buy this one, or
that one, they put up the money without the least hesitancy, relying upon
the superior judgement of their experienced companion to select that
which will best answer their purpose. Perhaps, by giving a history of the
"*inside workings*" of such cases, it may be the means of saving some gentleman of capital from being robbed out of a handsome commission in this
friendly manner. Now, it is frequently the case that this *experienced
friend* will tip the proprietor the wink and calling him aside, inquire in
an undertone what is the price of such an animal, and being informed of
the price, will say to the proprietor, "*Now, see here, I would like to make a
little out of this myself; this man don't care for the money; you just
add ten or twenty per cent. on your price for my commission, and I will
be instrumental in making a sale.*" In such cases the additional per cent.
always comes out of the pocket of the buyer, as the seller can well afford to
pay a handsome commission and still realize more from the sale of the animal than it is really worth. Now, the above I know to be facts, as I have
been approached on this subject and given to understand that by entering
into an arrangement of the above nature, would be the means of accom-
plishing a sale. I am happy to say, however, that *overtures of the above
kind are never made to me more than once by the same party*, and I am
well aware that in these instances I have missed making sales, but I have
the satisfaction of knowing that I have never been guilty of practicing this
system of robbery, and gentlemen who negotiate with me for any thing in

this catalogue, can rely upon one thing, and that is the price asked on all occasions is the *lowest dollar* that will buy the animal, and they are privileged to investigate the matter and see if my prices are not the same to all parties at that date; of course, where more than one animal is purchased, there may be some reduction made in the price.

In connection with the above, let me state here, for the benefit of that class of men who accompany gentlemen of means, with the expectation of robbing them whenever a favorably opportunity presents, THAT I PAY NO COMMISSIONS, and would advise them to waste none of their valuable time by calling at Forest Park.

In conclusion of this subject, let me say to gentlemen of capital, who never having had opportunities to become a good judge of horse flesh, and feeling that they cannot rely upon their own judgement, engage the services of some expert to counsel and select for them. I say, *be cautious gentlemen, as to whom you employ, and select only a man with whom you are personally acquainted and whose integrity is beyond question*, for, if you pick up a party here and there, you are liable to be robbed by your "*experienced*" friend.

It is not my desire to cast any reflection whatever upon the gentlemen engaged in the regular live stock commission business, for I have many friends engaged in this business who are reliable and honorable men, and their manner of conducting business is legitimate, and I can heartily endorse them as fair dealers and men upon whom the stranger can rely. The foregoing condemnatory remarks are intended solely for that class known in Kentucky as *Leggers* and *Backcappers* who, for the sake of making a few dollars out of the stranger (*who is unfortunate enough to fall into their hands*) will induce him to purchase that which they know to be worthless, and which is not what the purchaser is looking for. I EMPLOY NO "LEGGERS" EITHER AT HOME OR ABROAD, and when visitors come, if they feel they are not competent to select for themselves, let them bring some reliable and honest man of their acquaintance with them, and I have no fear but that my stock will show for themselves and be judged according to their merits, and should I have nothing to suit the visitors, I will feel satisfied in knowing that my stock have not been '*backcapped*," but have been inspected for what they are worth.

When I started in business I made it my motto never to refuse to price any thing I owned, and to make the rates asked on all occasions reasonable, so that no one would ever be able to say that he did not receive the value of his money. I expect to abide by these rules as long as I continue to trade and remain connected with my present calling.

The foregoing remarks will make it evident that everything in this catalogue is for sale. Moreover, I do not hesitate to say that the prices are as reasonable, and as much will be given at all times for the money as any similar establishment in the country, where animals are warranted as represented. With horses, as with most other commodities, the best are generally the cheapest; and the man who wants a first-rate article should at all times be willing to pay in proportion to quality ; and indeed, in these days, unless he is willing, the demand is such that he will have to go without. Take for example two colts of the same age. One of these might be cheap at $10,000 and the other dear at $200.

As I am constantly selling, so also I continue purchasing as opportunities offer, and thus keep up supply. I will keep on hand and for sale TROTTING PAIRS for gentlemen who desire driving teams, either for the road or track. And also persons wishing mares bought here in Kentucky, with a view to have them bred to any of my horses, can have my services in purchasing free of charge. I have frequently acted in this capacity, and the result in every case has been eminently satisfactory. This, which I confess is a source of much gratification, is due to the fact that I never buy for another what I would not buy for myself—for the same purpose.

It will be hardly necessary for me to add that every thing in this catalogue is believed to be correct and reliable in every particular; but should an error be found, and the proof be such as to convince me that it is not as represented, then no man will take greater interest or more pleasure in correcting it than   L. HERR.

REMARKS ON BREEDING THE TROTTER.

I will make a guess to see how it will hit it in 1890. Now the record is in favor of high bred ones—Maud S., 2:10¼, and Jay-Eye-See, 2:10¾, grandams thorougbred—and I predict that in 1890 the credit of the best record in repeating heats will still be in favor of a high bred one—that either the dam or grandam will be thoroughbred.

Some who are fighting high breeding may argue that the above were mere accidental hits; but the dam of Maud S , 2:10¼, also produced Nutwood, 2:18¾, and other good ones by different sires. Many others could be named that have a thoroughbred cross, either in the dam or grandam. There is no use squirming. it can't be got over, Maud S. and Jay-Eye-See (grandams thoroughbred), have beaten all the theories and crosses that have been made since the world began, either by judgement or accidental hits, to say nothing of the innumerable chances against it, very few until late years having had confidence to breed so high in blood. If the number of chances stood as much in favor of high breeding for the last fifty years, it would make a vast difference in favor of high breeding. It is like one chance against five thousand, and still the short side has beaten the long one.   Some have tried and failed ! reeding thoroughbred mares for trotters, starting on all pedigree and no mare.

My favorite foundation for trotters is a tried trotting sire to a thorough-bred mare of the right form and square gait, and that has produced a trotter herself in 2:30 or under, then we have a strictly thoroughbred mare (the dams of Fisk's Mambrino Chief and Lady Prewitt for example) and the trot to start on, and a good prospect for a trotter in the first or second produce.   I have now a select number of brood mares who have either dams or grandams thoroughbred, and in quality are an ormament to any breeding establishment.

ANNOUNCEMENT.

——o——

In view of the great and accumulating number of well bred trotting stallions, from all the popular families, and being located in all the States, I reduce the price of services of my stallions as follows:

MAMBRINO PATCHEN (full brother to Lady Thorn) . Insurance $100

SIR WALTER, record 2:25½, by Aberdeen . . . . Insurance   70

ARNOLD, by Goldsmith's Abdallah . . . . Insurance   50

MAMBRINO ABDALLAH, by Mambrino Patchen . . . Insurance   25

First-class pacing mares, and mares having produced trotters, or "trotters themselves," can be bred on the shares—colts equally divided at a year old.

Mares received and delivered, at any of the railroad depots, without charge.   All stock at owner's risk.

Mares kept on grass, and regularly attended to horses, at $5.00 per month.   My personal attention to all mares bred, &c.

SUCCESSFUL TROTTING SIRES

Must be uniform breeders, getting a great number of colts that can trot in three minutes or less, and frequently a first-class trotter.   We must breed where there are many prizes to the blanks.   It is bad policy to run or take the risk of breeding a valuable mare to a horse that breeds too many blanks in proportion to the prizes, only getting a trotter of note at long intervals, and probably never more than one or two, in a long life, from the most select mares. Mambrino Patchen has sired a stronger average of trotters under three minutes, down in the twenties, than any horse of his age I ever knew.

MAMBRINO PATCHEN MARES.

———o———

Mambrino Patchen mares, for brood mares, will be in greater demand than those of his noted sire, Mambrino Chief, whose get are so highly valued for brood mares, and are the dams and grandams of so many fast trotters. There are but few of Mambrino Chief's daughters now living, and they are old. The reason or proof for the above statement is that Mambrino Patchen has more in the 2:30 and under list than his sire "Mambrino Chief," breeds more style, and quality, better disposed, clearer of defects, more suitable for gentlemen's road horses, is sire of the finest stallion in the country, has sired more fine stallions and mares than any trotting stallion in Kentucky.

Since recording MAMBRINO PATCHEN, I have never applied to J. H. Wallace to record any of my stock, leaving it for buyers to record and name to suit themselves.

PACING MARES.

———o———

Mambrino Patchen makes many hits with pacing mares for speed, and gives them staying qualities, and what is remarkable, it does not matter how many gaits a mare has, pace, rack, trot, roll and tumble, every colt by Mambrino Patchen will trot square, getting the benefit of the pacing cross without having to change the gait from a pace to a trot, as they all come natural trotters.

MAMBRINO PATCHEN.

Black stallion, 16 hands.   Full brother to Lady Thorn, 2:18¼.

BY MAMBRINO CHIEF.

First dam, Lady Thorn's dam, 2:18¼, by Gano.

Second dam, by a son of Sir William, by Sir Archy, out of Bellona, by Bellair.

MAMBRINO CHIEF (sire of Lady Thorn, 2:18¼). by Mambrino Paymaster, son of Mambrino, by Imp. Messenger.

GANO. by American Eclipse, out of Betsey Richards, by Sir Archy, by Imp. Diomed.

SIR WILLIAM, by Sir Archy, son of Imp. Diomed; dam Transport, by Virginius, son of Sir Archy.

AMERICAN ECLIPSE, by Duroc, out of Miller's Damsel, by Imp. Messenger.

SIR WALTER.

[Record, 2:25½]

Chestnut stallion, 16 hands high; foaled 1873   Bred by Thos. Kilpatrick, N. Y.

BY ABERDEEN.

First dam, Lady Winfield, by Edward Everett.

Second dam, by Long Island Black Hawk.

Third dam, by Exton Eclipse

ABERDEEN (sire of Hattie Woodward, 2:15½, Hugh McLaughlin, 2:23, Kate Taylor, 2:23¾, &c.), got by Rysdyk's Hambletonian; dam Widow Machree, by American Star.

EDWARD EVERETT (sire of Judge Fullerton, 2:18, Sheridan, 2:20¼, Mountain Boy, 2:20¾, &c.), got by Rysdyk's Hambletonian, dam said to be by Imp. Margrave

LONG ISLAND BLACK HAWK (sire of Prince, 2:24½), got by Andrew Jackson; dam Sally Miller by Tippoo Saib.

No. 3.

ARNOLD.

Brown stallion, foaled 1875. Bred by T. J. Megibben.

BY GOLDSMITH'S ABDALLAH, 2:30.

First dam, Sallie Neal (dam of Hambrino Belle, 2:25½ at five years old), by Mambrino Chief.

Second dam, by Terror (thoroughbred).

Third dam, by Doublehead (thoroughbred).

Fourth dam, by American Eclipse.

GOLDSMITH'S ABDALLAH, 2:30, got by Volunteer, son of Rysdyk's Hambletonian ; dam Martha, by Abdallah, son of Mambrino; 2d dam by Conklin's Bellfounder, son of Imp. Bellfounder.

MAMBRINO CHIEF (sire of Lady Thorn, 2:18¼), got by Mambrino Paymaster, son of Mambrino, by Imp. Messenger.

VOLUNTEER, got by Rysdyk's Hambletonian; dam Lady Patriot, by Young Patriot.

No. 4.

MAMBRINO ABDALLAH.

Bay stallion, 15¾ hands, foaled 1873. Bred by L. Herr.

BY MAMBRINO PATCHEN.

First dam, Lady Ayres, by Redmon's Abdallah Patchen.

Second dam, Lady Abdallah (dam of Granville, 2:26), by Alexander's Abdallah.

MAMBRINO PATCHEN (full brother to Lady Thorn, 2:18¼), by Mambrino Chief; dam by Gano, son of American Eclipse; 2d dam by son of Sir William, by Sir Archy.

REDMON'S ABDALLAH PATCHEN, got by Alexander's Abdallah (sire of Goldsmith Maid, 2:14), son of Rysdyk's Hambletonian; dam Lady Valentine, by Redmon's Valentine, son of Imp. Valentine; 2d dam by Shakespeare; 3d dam by Potomac; 4th dam by Blackburn's Whip, son of Imp. Whip.

ALEXANDER'S ABDALLAH (sire of Goldsmith Maid, 2:14), got by Rysdyk's Hambletonian ; dam Katie Darling by Bay Roman.

No. 5.

SILVER KING.

Chestnut colt, foaled 1881. Bred by Herr & Scott.

BY MAMBRINO KING.

First dam, by Iron Duke.
Second dam, by Bay Messenger (Downing's).
Third dam, by Imp. Hooton.
Fourth dam, an old mare brought from Massachusetts, to Paris, Ky., that was a very fast and game road mare; pedigree not traced.

MAMBRINO KING, got by Mambrino Patchen; dam by Alexander's Edwin Forrest; 2d dam (the dam of Fisk's Mambrino Chief, 2:29½), by Birmingham; 3d dam by Bertrand; 4th dam by Sumpter; 5th dam by Imp. Buzzard.

IRON DUKE, got by Cassius M. Clay; dam by Young Cleveland; 2d dam by Bishop's Hambletonian; 3d dam by Commander, son of Imp. Messenger.

BAY MESSENGER, got by Harpinus, son of Hambletonian; dam of Messenger blood.

No. 6.

BOYNTON BOY.

Blood bay stallion, foaled 1879. Bred by Henry Buford.

BY VON ARNIM, 2:19¼.

First dam, Zora (the dam of St. Gothard, 2:29), by American Clay.
Second dam, Fillee, by John Dillard, son of Indian Chief.
Third dam, Molly Hunt, by Morgan Whip.
Fourth dam, by Lance, son of Ewing's Lance.
Fifth dam, Bettie Bounce (pacer).

VON ARNIM, 2:19¼, by Sentinel, son of Rysdyk's Hambletonian; dam May Short, by Blood's Black Hawk; 2d dam by Downing's Bay Messenger; 3d dam by Johnson's Star (thoroughbred).

AMERICAN CLAY, by Cassius M. Clay, Jr. (Strader's); dam by Imp. Tranby; 2d dam by Aratus, by Director.

THORN BOY.

[Full brother to Tillie Thorn].

Bay colt, foaled June 6th, 1882, two white feet behind.   Bred by L. Herr.

BY MAMBRINO PATCHEN.

First dam, Lady Ayres, by Redmon's Abdallah Patchen, by Alexander's Abdallah, sire of Goldsmith Maid, 2:14.

Second dam, Lady Abdallah (dam of Granville, 2:26), by Alexander's Abdallah.

MAMBRINO PATCHEN (full brother to Lady Thorn, 2:18¼), by Mambrino Chief; dam by Gano (son of American Eclipse); 2d dam by son of Sir William, by Sir Archy

REDMON'S ABDALLAH PATCHEN, got by Alexander's Abdallah, son of Rysdyk's Hambletonian; dam Lady Valentine, by Redmon's Valentine, son of Imp. Valentine; 2d dam by Shakespeare; 3d dam by Potomac; 4th dam by Blackburn's Whip, son of Imp. Whip.

ALEXANDER'S ABDALLAH (sire of Goldsmith Maid, 2:14), by Rysdyk's Hambletonian; dam Katy Darling, by Bay Roman.

CRIT DAVIS.

Chestnut colt, both hind feet and right front white, star in forehead; foaled April 25, 1882.   Bred by L. Herr.

BY CRITTENDEN (trial 2:29).

First dam, Sunnyside, by Richelieu.

Second dam, Abdallah Belle, by Gum Elastic.

Third dam, Lady Abdallah (dam of Granville, 2:26), by Alexander's Abdallah, by Rysdyk's Hambletonian.

CRITTENDEN (sire of Mamie M., 2:25, and Josie H., 2:32½), got by Strader's Cassius M. Clay, Jr., son of Cassius M. Clay; dam

Flora, by Pilot, Jr.; 2d dam Mary (dam of Dick Moore, 2:22½), by Monmouth Eclipse.

RICHELIEU, by Hiawatha, dam Fanny McAllister, by O'Meara; 2d dam by Imp. Leviathan.

GUM ELASTIC, by American Clay, son of Strader's Cassius M. Clay, Jr.; dam Laytham Lass, by Alexander's Abdallah; 2d dam by Mambrino Chief; 3d dam by Bellfounder.

ALEXANDER'S ABDALLAH (sire of Goldsmith Maid, 2:14) by Rysdyk's Hambletonian; dam Katy Darling, by Bay Roman.

No. 9.

BALTIMORE.

Dark bay colt, foaled 1880.   Bred by L. Herr.

BY MAMBRINO KING.

First dam, by a son of Red Eye, by Boston.
Second dam, by a son of old St. Lawrence.

MAMBRINO KING, got by Mambrino Patchen; dam by Alexander's Edwin Forrest; 2d dam (the dam of Fisk's Mambrino Chief), by Birmingham; 3d dam by Bertrand; 4th dam by Sumpter, by Sir Archy; 5th dam by Imp. Buzzard.

RED EYE, four mile race horse, by old Boston, sire of Lexington.

ST. LAWRENCE, a noted trotter.

No. 10.

MAMBRINO GOLDSMITH.

Black colt, foaled April 26th, 1882.   Bred by Alex McClintock, Millersburg. Ky.

BY MAMBRINO PATCHEN.

First dam, Mambrino Kate, by Goldsmith.
Second dam, by Rutzer's Mambrino Messenger.
Third dam, by Washington.
Fourth dam, by Mount Holly.

MAMBRINO PATCHEN (brother to Lady Thorn, 2:18¼), by Mam-

brino Chief; dam by Gano, son of American Eclipse; 2d dam by
son of Sir William.

GOLDSMITH, by Rysdyk's Hambletonian; dam by Imp. Trustee; 2d
dam Emma, by Whisker, by Waxy.

RUTZER'S MAMBRINO MESSENGER, by Dunkin's Mambrino Messenger; dam by son of Imp. Bussorah, Arabian.

WASHINGTON, by Mambrino Paymaster, son of Mambrino, by Imp.
Messenger; dam by Mount Holly, son of Imp. Messenger.

No. 11.

HAMLIN KING.

Sorrel colt, foaled March 25th, 1882. Bred E. D. Herr.

BY MAMBRINO KING.

First dam Maggie Marshall, by Bradford's Telegraph.
Second dam by Prince Richard, thoroughbred.

MAMBRINO KING, got by Mambrino Patchen; dam by Alexander's
Edwin Forrest; 2d dam (the dam of Fisk's Mambrino Chief,
2:29¼), by Birmingham; 3d dam by Bertrand; 4th dam by
Sumpter; 5th dam by Imp. Buzzard.

TELEGRAPH, got by Vermont Black Hawk, son of Sherman Morgan;
dam by Vermont Hambletonian.

VERMONT HAMBLETONIAN, got by Harris' Hambletonian; dam by
Comet, son of Bishop's Hambletonian.

No. 12.

PIONEER BOY.

Sorrel colt, star in face, foaled 1881. Bred by Herr and Robb.

BY MAMBRINO PATCHEN.

First dam by Young America.
Second dam by Pioneer, by Cook's Whip.

MAMBRINO PATCHEN (full brother to Lady Thorn, 2:18¼), by Mambrino Chief; dam by Gano, son of American Eclipse; 2d dam by
a son of Sir William, by Sir Archy.

VERSAILLES BOY.

Bay colt, star and right hind foot white, foaled April 20th, 1882.
Bred by L. Herr.

BY MAMBRINO ABDALLAH.

First dam Versailles Maid, by Hurst & Thornton's Abdallah, by Alexander's Abdallah.

Second dam by Paddy Burns, by Grey Eagle.

MAMBRINO ABDALLAH, got by Mambrino Patchen; dam Lady Ayres, by Redmon's Abdallah Patchen, son of Alexander's Abdallah; 2d dam Lady Abdallah (dam of Granville, 2:26), by Alexander's Abdallah.

HURST & THORNTON'S ABDALLAH, got by Alexander's Abdallah (sire of Goldsmith Maid, 2:14); dam by St. Lawrence.

BRADFORD.

Brown colt, foaled 1882. Bred by T. Pollock.

BY MAMBRINO KING.

First dam by Bradford's Telegraph.

Second dam by Marsden (thoroughbred).

Third dam by Ivanhoe (thoroughbred).

MAMBRINO KING, got by Mambrino Patchen; dam by Alexander's Edwin Forrest; 2d dam (the dam of Fisk's Mambrino Chief, 2:29½), by Birmingham; 3d dam by Bertrand; 4th dam by Sumpter; 5th dam by Imp. Buzzard.

TELEGRAPH (Bradford's), got by Vermont Black Hawk, son of Sherman Morgan; dam by Vermont Hambletonian.

VERMONT HAMBLETONIAN, got by Harris' Hambletonian; dam by Comet, son of Bishop's Hambletonian.

No. 15.

CURTIS.

Sorrel colt, foaled 1882. Bred by Jno. Curtis.

BY MAMBRINO KING.

First dam by Mambrino Patchen.
Second dam by Delmonico.

MAMBRINO KING, got by Mambrino Patchen; dam by Alexander's
Edwin Forrest; 2d dam (the dam of Fisk's Mambrino Chief,
2:29½), by Birmingham; 3d dam by Bertrand; 4th dam by
Sumpter; 5th dam by Imp. Buzzard.

MAMBRINO PATCHEN (brother to Lady Thorn, 2:18¼), got by Mambrino Chief; dam by Gano, son of American Eclipse; 2d dam
by son of Sir William, by Sir Archy.

DELMONICO (sire of Darby, 2:16½), got by Guy Miller, son of Rysdyk's
Hambletonian; dam Harvey Adams mare, by Rysdyk's Hambletonian; 2d dam, by Imp. Bellfounder.

No. 16.

INDIAN BOY.

Chestnut Colt, right hind ankle white and blaze face; foaled
April 18th, 1883. Bred by L. Herr.

BY MAMBRINO KING.

First dam Lydia Ann, by Indian Chief (sire of Warrior, 2:26).
Second dam by Redmon's Valentine, son of Imp. Valentine.

MAMBRINO KING, got by Mambrino Patchen; dam by Alexander's
Edwin Forrest; 2d dam (the dam of Fisk's Mambrino Chief,
2:29½), by Birmingham; 3d dam by Bertrand; 4th dam by
Sumpter, by Sir Archy; 5th dam by Imp. Buzzard.

INDIAN CHIEF (sire of Warrior, 2:26), got by Blood's Black Hawk, son
of Vermont Black Hawk; dam Lou Berry, by Ned Forrest, son
of Young Bashaw; 2d dam Fan, by Tucker's Grey Messenger.

REDMON'S VALENTINE, got by Imp. Valentine.

JACKSON,

Bay Colt, foaled June 20, 1883, left hind foot white.   Bred by
L. Herr.

BY MAMBRINO ABDALLAH.

First dam Fanny Haserack, by Washington Denmark, by Old Denmark.
Second dam, by Haserack, a Copperbottom horse.

MAMBRINO ABDALLAH, got by Mambrino Patchen : dam, Lady
Ayres, by Redmon's Abdallah Patchen, son of Alexander's Abdallah; 2d dam, Lady Abdallah (dam of Granville, 2:26), by Alexander's Abdallah.

TRAVELER.

Sorrel Colt, foaled April 24, 1883.   Bred by Hugh Huntington,
Ohio,

BY HAPPY TRAVELER, 2:27½.

First dam, Madaline Mambrino, by Mambrino Patchen.
Second dam, Arabian Belle, by Imp. Fysaul, Arabian.
Third dam, Sultana, Arabian.
Fourth dam, Old Sultana, Arabian, &c.

HAPPY TRAVELER, 2:27½, got by Baird's Hambletonian Prince, son of
Rysdyk's Hambletonian; dam, Lady Larkin, by Little Jack, son of
Long Island Black Hawk; 2d dam, by Long Island Black Hawk;
3d dam, by Bay Messenger Duroc.

HAMBLETONIAN PRINCE (Baird's), got by Rysdyk's Hambletonian;
dam, Nellie Cammeyer, by Cassius M. Clay; 2d dam, by Chancel-
lor, son of Mambrino.

MAMBRINO PATCHEN (brother to Lady Thorn, 2:18¼), by Mambrino Chief ; dam, by Gano, son of American Eclipse; 2d dam, by
son of Sir William, by Sir Archy.

LARABIE.

Bay Colt, foaled April 3d, 1883; star and two white hind feet.
Bred by L. Herr.

BY MAXIM (son of Belmont).

First dam, Versailles Maid, by Hurst & Thornton's Abdallah.
Second dam, by Paddy Burns, by Grey Eagle.

MAXIM, got by Belmont (sire of Nutwood, 2:18¼), son of Alexander's Abdallah; dam, Primrose (the dam of Princeps, sire of Trinket, 2:14), by Alexander's Abdallah; 2d dam, Black Rose (dam of Darkness, 2:27¾), by Tom Teemer; 3d dam, by Cannon's Whip; 4th dam, by Robin Grey.

HURST & THORNTON'S ABDALLAH, got by Alexander's Abdallah (sire of Goldsmith Maid. 2:14), son of Rysdyk's Hambletonian; dam, by St. Lawrence.

PADDY BURNS, by Grey Eagle, &c.

SPRAGUE.

Black Colt, foaled April 25th, 1883. Two white hind feet.
Bred by L. Herr.

BY GOV. SPRAGUE, 2:20½.

First dam, King's Beauty, by Mambrino King.
Second dam, by Glencoe, Jr., by Imp. Glencoe.
Third dam, by Lexington, by Boston.
Fourth dam, by Ruffian.
Fifth dam, by Leviathan
Sixth dam, by Stockholder.
Seventh dam, by Pacolet.
Eighth dam, by Imp. Citizen.

GOV. SPRAGUE, 2:20½ (sire of Kate Sprague, 2:18), got by Rhode Island; dam, Belle Brandon, by Rysdyk's Hambletonian; 2d dam, Jenny, by Young Bacchus; 3d dam, by Exton Eclipse.

MAMBRINO KING, got by Mambrino Patchen; dam, by Alexander's Edwin Forrest; 2d dam (the dam of Fisk's Mambrino Chief, 2:29½) by Birmingham; 3d dam, by Bertrand; 4th dam, by Sumpter, by Sir Archy; 5th dam, by Imp. Buzzard.

JOHN M. CLAY.

Dark Gray Colt, foaled 1883; right hind foot white.   Bred by
John M. Clay.

BY MAMBRINO ABDALLAH.

First dam, by Mambrino Chorister, sire of the dam of Proteine, 2:18;
Belle Brasfield, 2:20, and Belle Patchen, 2:30¾.

MAMBRINO ABDALLAH, got by Mambrino Patchen; dam, Lady
Ayres, by Redmon's Abdallah Patchen, son of Alexander's Abdallah; 2d dam, Lady Abdallah (dam of Granville, 2:26), by Alexander's Abdallah.

MAMBRINO CHORISTER (sire of the dam of Proteine, 2:18; Belle Brasfield, 2:20, and Belle Patchen, 2:30¾), got by Mambrino Chief;
dam by Chorister; 2d dam, by Medley.

MARES AND FILLIES.

TILLIE THORN.

Bay Mare, foaled 1876.   Bred by L. Herr.

BY MAMBRINO PATCHEN.

In foal to Arnold.

First dam, Lady Ayres, by Redmon's Abdallah Patchen.
Second dam, Lady Abdallah (dam of Granville, 2:26), by Alexander's
Abdallah.

ARNOLD, got by Goldsmith's Abdallah, 2:30, son of Volunteer; dam,
Sally Neal (dam of Hambrino Belle, 2:25½), by Mambrino Chief,
&c.

MAMBRINO PATCHEN (brother to Lady Thorn, 2:18¼), by Mambrino Chief; dam, by Gano, son of American Eclipse; 2d dam, by
Son of Sir William, &c.

REDMON'S ABDALLAH PATCHEN, got by Alexander's Abdallah

(sire of Goldsmith Maid, 2:14), son of Rysdyk's Hambletonian; dam Lady Valentine, by Redmon's Valentine, son of Imp. Valentine; 2d dam, by Shakespeare; 3d dam, by Potomac; 4th dam, by Black-burn's Whip, son of Imp. Whip.

ALEXANDER'S ABDALLAH (sire of Goldsmith Maid, 2·14), got by Rysdyk's Hambletonian; dam, Katy Darling, by Bay Roman.

No. 23.

LUCY MONAHAN.

[Formerly Fairy. Record, 2:35¼; trial, 2:27].

Black Mare, foaled April 26, 1875. Bred by H. G. Starr, Carey, Ohio.

BY ROBERT FILLINGHAM, JR., SON OF GEO. WILKES.

First dam, Silver Cloud, by Orr's Flying Cloud, son of Hill's Vermont Black Hawk.

Second dam, "Het," by the Johnson horse, of Tiffin, Ohio, claimed to be by a thoroughbred from Maryland.

Third dam, "Pop," by Hayman's Messenger, a gray horse taken to Ohio from New York in 1832. All of the above dams were bred and raised by H. J. Starr, of Carey, Ohio.

ROBERT FILLINGHAM, Jr., got by George Wilkes (sire of So-So, 2:17¼; Rosa Wilkes, 2:18¼, &c.); dam, Ohio Maid, a bay mare taken from Columbus, Ohio, to Orange County, N. Y., and was claimed to be by Taylor's Bellfounder, son of Brown's Bellfounder.

ORR'S FLYING CLOUD (bred by Gustavus Wicks, Ticonderoga, N. Y.) by Hill's Vermont Black Hawk; dam a Magnum Bonum mare.

No. 24.

BESSIE HUNTINGTON.

Bay Filly, foaled 1882. Bred by Hugh Huntington, Ohio.

BY HAPPY TRAVELER, 2:27½.

First dam, Madaline Mambrino, by Mambrino Patchen.
Second dam, Arabian Belle, by Imp. Fysaul, Arabian.

Third dam, Sultana, Arabian.

Fourth dam, Old Sultana, Arabian.

HAPPY TRAVELER, 2:27½, by Baird's Hambletonian Prince, son of
Rysdyk's Hambletonian; dam, Lady Larkin, by Little Jack, son of
Long Island Black Hawk; 2d dam, by Long Island Black Hawk;
3d dam, by Bay Messenger Duroc.

HAMBLETONIAN PRINCE (Baird's), got by Rysdyk's Hambletonian;
dam, Nelly Cammeyer, by Cassius M. Clay; 2d dam, by Chancel-
lor, son of Mambrino.

MAMBRINO PATCHEN (brother to Lady Thorn, 2:18¼), by Mambrino
Chief; dam, by Gano, son of American Eclipse; 2d dam, by Son
of Sir Willian, by Sir Archy.

No. 25.

MODEL GIRL.

Bay Filly, left hind foot white, foaled 1882.   Bred by Herr &
Capt. Jackson.

BY MAMBRINO KING.

First dam, Fanny Haserack, by Washington Denmark.

Second dam, by Haserack, of Copperbotton stock.

MAMBRINO KING, by Mambrino Patchen; dam, by Alexander's Edwin
Forrest; 2d dam (the dam of Fisk's Mambrino Chief, 2:29½), by
Birmingham; 3d dam, by Bertrand; 4th dam, by Sumpter, by Sir
Archy; 5th dam, by Imp. Buzzard.

No. 26.

ALFARETTA.

Bay Filly, foaled May 13th, 1882.   Bred by L. Herr.

BY MAMBRINO KING.

First dam, Silver Lake, by Lakeland Abdallah.

Second dam, Alice, by the Imp. Knight of St. George.

Third dam, Bellamira, by Imp. Monarch.
Fourth dam, Kitty Heath, by American Eclipse.
Fifth dam, Pomona, by Sir Alfred.
Sixth dam, by Imp. Sir Harry.
Seventh dam, Imp. Pomona, by Worthy.
Eight dam, Comedy, by Buzzard.

MAMBRINO KING, by Mambrino Patchen (brother to Lady Thorn, 2:18¼); dam, by Alexander's Edwin Forrest; 2d dam (the dam of Fisk's Mambrino Chief, 2:29½), by Birmingham; 3d dam, by Bertrand; 4th dam, by Sumpter; 5th dam, by Imp. Buzzard.

LAKELAND ABDALLAH (brother to Harold, sire of Maud S., 2:10¼) got by Rysdyk's Hambletonian; dam, Enchantress, by Abdallah.

No. 27.

GUERRILLA.

Bay Mare, foaled 1880.   Bred by George M. Jewett, Ohio.

BY ALMONT CHIEF.

First dam, Lucy Luby, by Dolphin, by Pataskala.
Second dam, Guerrilla (pacer), who could pace in 2:22.

ALMONT CHIEF, got by Almont (sire of Piedmont, 2:17¼; Fanny Witherspoon, 2:17; Aldine, 2:19¼, &c); dam, Monogram, by Mambrino Chief; 2d dam, a fine mare taken from South Carolina to Kentucky.

ALMONT, got by Alexander's Aballah; dam, by Mambrino Chief; 2d dam, by Pilot, Jr.

No. 28.

ROSE BUD.

Chestnut Mare, foaled 1880.   Bred by A. G. Hunt.

BY MAMBRINO KING.

First dam, Fanny, by Blood's Black Hawk.

Second dam, by Berthune.

Third dam, Hunt's premium mare, by Scott's Highlander.

MAMBRINO KING, by Mambrino Patchen; dam, by Alexander's Edwin
Forrest; 2d dam (the dam of Fisk's Mambrino Chief, 2:29½), by
Birmingham; 3d dam, by Bertrand; 4th dam, by Sumpter, by Sir
Archy; 5th dam, by Imp. Buzzard.

BLOOD'S BLACK HAWK, son of Vermont Black Hawk.

BERTHUNE, thoroughbred.

SCOTT'S HIGHLANDER, by Hunt's Brown Highlander; dam, a Whit-
tington mare.

No. 29

BLACK FAWN.

Black Filly, foaled June 14th, 1881.   Bred by U. M. Morgan,
Ohio.

BY MAMBRINO MORGAN (full brother to the Jewess, 2:26), by Mambrino Patchen.

First dam, Gold Drop, by Mambrino Patchen.

Second dam, Lady Wallenstein (dam of Lady Prewitt, 2:30, and also
dam of the winner of the Newmarket Handicap in 1879 and 1880),
by Lexington.

Third dam, Louisa, by Imp. Yorkshire.

Fourth dam, by American Eclipse.

Fifth dam, Nell, by Orphan.

Sixth dam, by Imp. Buzzard.

MAMBRINO MORGAN, got by Mambrino Patchen; dam, Letitia (the
dam of the Jewess, 2:26), by Miller's Joe Downing, son of Alexander's Edwin Forrest; 2d dam, by Herr's Cœur de Lion, Canadian,
son of Cœur de Lion.

MAMBRINO PATCHEN (full brother to Lady Thorn, 2:18¼), by Mambrino Chief ; dam, by Gano, son of American Eclipse; 2d dam, by
son of Sir William, &c.

No. 30.

BALTIMORE GIRL.

Bay Filly, left hind foot white. foaled July 3d, 1882.   Bred by
L. Herr.

BY MAMBRINO ABDALLAH.

First dam Molly Linthicum, by a son of Red Eye, he by Boston.
Second dam by a son of Old St. Lawrence.

MAMBRINO ABDALLAH. by Mambrino Patchen; dam Lady Ayres,
by Redmon's Abdallah Patchen, son of Alexander's Abdallah; 2d
dam, Lady Abdallah (dam of Granville, 2:26). by Alexander's Abdallah.

    •

No. 31.

MAGGIE GUNN.

Black Filly, gray hairs mixed in coat, foaled March 25, 1883.
Bred by L. Herr.

BY ALCYONE, 2:27 (brother to Alcantara, 2:23).

First dam, Girlie Gunn. by Mambrino Patchen.
Second dam, by Lightning.
Third dam, by Grey Eagle.
Fourth dam, by Blackburn's Whip.

ALCYONE, 2:27 (full brother to Alcantara, 2:23), by George Wilkes (son
of Rysdyk's Hambletonian) ; dam, Alma Mater, by Mambrino
Patchen; 2d dam. Estella. by Imp. Australian; 3d dam, Fanny G.,
by Imp. Margrave; 4th dam, Miss Lancess, by Lance, &c.

MAMBRINO PATCHEN. got by Mambrino Chief; dam (Lady Thorn's
dam). by Gano; 2d dam by a son of Sir William.

LIGHTNING, by Lexington, by Boston, &c.

GREY EAGLE, by Woodpecker, by Bertrand.

BLACKBURN'S WHIP, by Imp. Whip.

JENNIE WILKES.

Sorrel Filly, foaled July 5th, 1883. Bred by L. Herr.

BY RED WILKES (sire of Phil Thompson, record at three years old, 2:21).

First dam, Gold Penn, by Mambrino Abdallah, by Mambrino Patchen.
Second dam, by Harold (sire of Maud S., 2:10¼).
Third dam, by Mambrino Patchen (sire of London, 2:20½).
Fourth dam, by Snowstorm (Wilson's), sire of Jim Irving, 2:23.
Fifth dam, by Wagner (thoroughbred).

RED WILKES (sire of Phil Thompson, 2:21, at three years old), by Geo.
Wilkes; dam, Queen Dido, by Mambrino Chief; 2d dam, by Red
Jacket, son of Comet.

MAMBRINO ABDALLAH, got by Mambrino Patchen; dam, Lady
Ayres, by Redmon's Abdallah Patchen, son of Alexander's Abdallah; 2d dam. Lady Abdallah (dam of Granville, 2:26), by Alexander's Abdallah.

HAROLD (sire of Maud S., 2:10¼), got by Rysdyk's Hambletonian; dam,
Enchantress, by Abdallah, &c.; 2d dam, by Imp. Bellfounder.

MAMBRINO PATCHEN (brother to Lady Thorn, 2:18¼), by Mambrino Chief; dam, by Gano, son of American Eclipse; 2d dam, by
a son of Sir William, by Sir Archy, &c.

SNOWSTORM (sire of Jim Irving, 2:23), got by Steele's Snowstorm, pacer;
dam, by Sidi Hamet, son of Virginian; 2d dam, by Phillips' Tippoo
Saib; 3d dam, by Hamilton.

LOU PORTER.

Sorrel Filly, foaled March 15th, 1883; star and two white hind
feet. Bred by E. D. Herr.

BY MAMBRINO KING.

First dam, Maggie Marshall, by Bradford's Telegraph.
Second dam, by Prince Richard, thoroughbred.

MAMBRINO KING, got by Mambrino Patchen; dam, by Alexander's Edwin Forrest; 2d dam (the dam of Fisk's Mambrino Chief, 2:29½), by Birmingham; 3d dam, by Bertrand; 4th dam, by Sumpter; 5th dam, by Imp. Buzzard.

TELEGRAPH (Bradford's), got by Vermont Black Hawk, son of Sherman Morgan; dam by Vermont Hambletonian.

VERMONT HAMBLETONIAN, got by Harris' Hambletonian; dam, by Comet, son of Bishop's Hambletonian.

No. 34.

MAXIM BEAUTY.

Bay Filly, foaled April 22d, 1883; star and right hind ankle white. Bred by L. Herr.

BY MAXIM (son of Belmont).

First dam, King Girl, by Mambrino King.
Second dam, Leah (trial 2:26), by Wilson's Blue Bull.
Third dam, by Tom Hal (pacer).

MAXIM, got by Belmont (sire of Nutwood, 2:18¼), son of Alexander's Abdallah; dam, Primrose (the dam of Princeps, sire of Trinket, 2:14), by Alexander's Abdallah.

MAMBRINO KING, got by Mambrino Patchen, dam, by Alexander's Edwin Forrest; 2d dam (the dam of Fisk's Mambrino Chief, 2:29½), by Birmingham; 3d dam, by Bertrand; 4th dam, by Sumpter, by Sir Archy; 5th dam, by Imp. Buzzard.

BLUE BULL (Wilson's), got by Pruden's Blue Bull; dam, not traced.

No. 35.

BLUE EYES.

Black Filly, foaled April 3d, 1882. Bred by L. P. Herr.

BY MAMBRINO KING.

First dam, Molly, by Bald Stockings, pacer.

MAMBRINO KING, by Mambrino Patchen; dam, by Alexander's Edwin Forrest; 2d dam (the dam of Fisk's Mambrino Chief, 2:29½), by Birmingham; 3d dam, by Bertrand; 4th dam, by Sumpter, &c.

BALD STOCKINGS (pacer), by Tom Hal (pacer); dam, by Chinn's Copperbottom; 2d dam, by Tarquin.

STYLE.

Bay Filly, foaled April 20th, 1883; right hind foot white. Bred by L. Herr.

BY MAXIM, (son of Belmont).

First dam, Sunnyside, by Richelieu.

Second dam, Abdallah Belle, by Gum Elastic.

Third dam, Lady Abdallah (dam of Granville, 2:26), by Alexander's Abdallah, &c.

MAXIM, got by Belmont (sire of Nutwood, 2:18¼), son of Alexander's Abdallah; dam, Primrose (the dam of Princeps, sire of Trinket, 2:14), by Alexander's Abdallah.

RICHELIEU (thoroughbred), got by Hiawatha; dam, Fanny McAllister, by O'Meara; 2d dam, by Imp. Leviathan, &c.

GUM ELASTIC, got by American Clay; dam, Latham Lass, by Alexanander's Abdallah; 2d dam, by Mambrino Chief; 3d dam, by Bellfounder.

ALEXANDER'S ABDALLAH (sire of Goldsmith Maid, 2:14), got by Rysdyk's Hambletonian; dam, Katy Darling. by Bay Roman.

FINEST OF ALL.

Chestnut Filly, foaled April 2d, 1883; star and small snip. Bred by L. Herr.

BY MAMBRINO KING.

First dam, Golden Lake, by Lakeland Abdallah.

Second dam, Alice, by the Imp. Knight of St. George.

Third dam, Bellamira, by Imp. Monarch.

Fourth dam, Kitty Heath, by American Eclipse.

Fifth dam, Pomona, by Sir Alfred.

Sixth dam, by Imp Sir Harry.

Seventh dam, Imp. Pomona, by Worthy.

Eighth dam, Comedy, by Buzzard.

MAMBRINO KING, got by Mambrino Patchen; dam, by Alexander's Ed-

win Forrest; 2d dam (the dam of Fisk's Mambrino Chief, 2:29½),
by Birmingham; 3d dam, by Bertrand; 4th dam, by Sumpter, by
Sir Archy; 5th dam, by Imp. Buzzard.

LAKELAND ABDALLAH (full brother to Harold, sire of Maud S.,
2:10¼), by Rysdyk's Hambletonian; dam, Enchantress, by Abdal
lah; 2d dam, by Imp. Bellfounder.

No. 38.

JUST RIGHT.

Dark Brown Filly, foaled 1883; right hind pastern white. Bred
by Herr and Edwin S. Young.

BY MAMBRINO PATCHEN.

First dam, by Honest Allen (2:33½) sire of Prince Allen, 2:26½.
Second dam, by Donerail (thoroughbred), by Lexington.

MAMBRINO PATCHEN (full brother to Lady Thorn, 2:18¼), by Mambrino Chief; dam, by Gano, son of American Eclipse; 2d dam, by
a son of Sir William, by Sir Archy, &c.

HONEST ALLEN, got by Ethan Allen; dam, Edgerly mare, by the
Brooks Horse, son of Sherman Morgan; 2d dam, by Cock of the
Rock.

No. 39.

PUNCHEY.

Brown Filly, foaled 1881.   Bred by Dr. Seys, Ohio.

SIRED BY A DRAUGHT STALLION.

First dam, Play Girl, by Mambrino Patchen.
Second dam, the Johnson Coons mare, by a son of Vandal (who was
bred by George Coons), out of Gyp, by Old Abdallah; 2d dam, by
Potomac; 3d dam, by Buzzard; 4th dam, by Diomed.
Third dam, the Felton mare, who could trot in 2:40; pedigree not traced.

BROOD MARES.

HECLA.

Bay mare, foaled 1873. Bred by Dan Swigert.

BY ALMONT.

In foal to Nugget.

First dam Haidee, by Mambrino Chief.
Second dam by Zenith.
Third dam Lucy Alexander, by Alexander.
Fourth dam by Moses.
Fifth dam by Duke of Bedford.
Sixth dam by Union.
Seventh dam by Dabster.

ALMONT (sire of Fanny Witherspoon, 2:17, Piedmont, 2:17¼, Aldine. 2:19¼). by Alexander's Abdallah, son of Rysdyk's Hambletonian; dam by Mambrino Chief; 2d dam by Pilot, Jr.

MAMBRINO CHIEF (sire of Lady Thorn, 2:18¼), by Mambrino Paymaster, son of Mambrino, by Imp. Messenger.

NUGGET, got by Wedgewood, 2:19; dam Minerva, by Pilot, Jr.; 2d dam Bacchante Mambrino, by Mambrino Chief; 3d dam Bacchante, by Downing's Bay Messenger; 4th dam by Whip Comet; 5th dam by Grey Messenger.

WEDGEWOOD, 2:19, got by Belmont (sire of Nutwood, 2:18¾); dam Woodbine (the dam of Woodford Mambrino, 2:21½), by Woodford.

BELMONT, by Alexander's Abdallah (sire of Goldsmith Maid, 2:14); dam Belle, by Mambrino Chief; 2d dam by Brown's Bellfounder.

The produce of Hecla will embrace the following trotting elements in the pedigree: Four crosses of Mambrino Chief; two crosses of Abdallah or Hambletonian; two crosses of Pilot. Jr., and also thoroughbred.

GOLD PENN.

Bay mare, foaled 1879. Bred by Logan Railey.

Bred late to Dictator.

BY MAMBRINO ABDALLAH.

First dam by Harold (sire of Maud S., 2:10¼).
Second dam by Mambrino Patchen, brother to Lady Thorn, 2:18¼.
Third dam by Snowstorm (Wilson's) sire of Jim Irving, 2:23.
Fourth dam by Wagner.

MAMBRINO ABDALLAH, got by Mambrino Patchen; dam Lady
    Ayres, by Redmon's Abdallah Patchen, son of Alexander's Ab-
    dallah; 2d dam Lady Abdallah (dam of Granville, 2:26), by Alex-
    ander's Abdallah.

HAROLD (sire of Maud S., 2:10¼), got by Rysdyk's Hambletonian; dam
    Enchantress, by Abdallah; 2d dam by Imp. Bellfounder.

MAMBRINO PATCHEN (full brother to Lady Thorn, 2:18¼), by Mam-
    brino Chief; dam by Gano, son of American Eclipse; 2d dam by
    a son of Sir William, by Sir Archy.

SNOWSTORM (sire of Jim Irving, 2:23), got by Steele's Snowstorm
    (pacer) : dam by Sidi Hamet, son of Virginian; 2d dam by
    Phillips' Tippoo Saib; 3d dam by Hamilton.

GIRL E. QUEEN.

[Record, at three years old, 2:33¼].

Dark brown mare, foaled 1872. Bred by W. W. Adams.

BY MAMBRINO PATCHEN.

In foal to Arnold.

First dam by Dixie, by A. K Richards' Imp. Arabian Mokhladi.
Second dam by Stockholder
Third dam by Sumpter, by Sir Archy.

ARNOLD, by Goldsmith's Abdallah, 2:30, son of Volunteer; dam Sally
    Neal (dam of Hambrino Belle, 2:25½), by Mambrino Chief.

MAMBRINO PATCHEN (brother to Lady Thorn, 2:18¼), by Mam-
    brino Chief; dam by Gano, son of American Eclipse ; 2d dam
    by son of Sir William, by Sir Archy.

LUCY DOLE.

Bay Filly, foaled 1880. Bred by L. Herr.

BY MAMBRINO ABDALLAH.

In foal to Arnold.

First dam Silver Lake, by Lakeland Abdallah.
Second dam Alice. by Imp. Knight of St. George.
Third dam Bellamira, by Imp. Monarch.
Fourth dam Kitty Heath, by American Eclipse.
Fifth dam Pomona, by Sir Alfred.
Sixth dam by Imp. Sir Harry.
Seventh dam Imp. Pomona, by Worthy.
Eighth dam Comedy, by Buzzard.

ARNOLD, by Goldsmith's Abdallah, 2:30, son of Volunteer; dam Sally
Neal (the dam of Hambrino Belle. 2:25½), by Mambrino Chief.

MAMBRINO ABDALLAH, got by Mambrino Patchen ; dam Lady
Ayres, by Redmon's Abdallah Patchen, son of Alexander's Ab-
dallah; 2d dam Lady Abdallah (dam of Granville, 2:26), by
Alexander's Abdallah.

LAKELAND ABDALLAH (brother to Harold, sire of Maud S., 2:10¼)'
got by Rysdyk's Hambletonian; dam Enchantress, by Abdallah,
2d dam by Imp. Bellfounder.

GOLDEN LAKE.

Bay Mare, foaled 1874. Bred by C. S. Dole, Ill.

BY LAKELAND ABDALLAH (full brother to Harold sire of Maud
S., 2:10¼).

In foal to Mambrino Patchen.

First dam Alice, by Imp. Knight of St George.
Second dam Bellamira, by Imp. Monarch.
Third dam Kitty Heath, by American Eclipse.
Fourth dam Pomona by Sir Alfred.
Fifth dam by Imp. Sir Harry.

Sixth dam Imp. Pomona, by Worthy.
Seventh dam Comedy, by Buzzard.

MAMBRINO PATCHEN (brother to Lady Thorn, 2:18¼), by Mambrino
Chief; dam by Gano, son of American Eclipse; 2d dam by son
of Sir William, by Sir Archy.

LAKELAND ABDALLAH (brother to Harold, sire of Maud S., 2:10¼),
got by Rysdyk's Hambletonian ; dam Enchantress, by Abdallah;
2d dam by Imp. Bellfounder.

No. 45.

SILVER LAKE.

Bay Mare, foaled 1875. Bred by C. S. Dole, Ills.

BY LAKELAND ABDALLAH (full brother to Harold, sire of Maud
S., 2:10¼).

In foal to Mambrino Patchen.

First dam Alice, by Imp. Knight of St. George.
Second dam Bellamira, by Imp. Monarch.
Third dam Kitty Heath, by American Eclipse.
Fourth dam Pomona, by Sir Alfred.
Fifth dam by Imp. Sir Harry.
Sixth dam Imp. Pomona, by Worthy.
Seventh dam Comedy, by Buzzard.

MAMBRINO PATCHEN (brother to Lady Thorn, 2:18¼), by Mambrino
Chief; dam by Gano, son of American Eclipse; 2d dam by son
of Sir William, by Sir Archy.

LAKELAND ABDALLAH (brother to Harold, sire of Maud S , 2:10¼),
got by Rysdyk's Hambletonian ; dam Enchantress, by Abdallah;
2d dam by Imp. Bellfounder.

LADY AYRES.

Bay Mare, toaled 1865. Bred by Herman Ayres, Bourbon county, Ky.

BY REDMON'S ABDALLAH PATCHEN.

In foal to Mambrino Patchen.

First dam Lady Abdallah (dam of Granville, 2.26), by Alexander's Abdallah (sire of Goldsmith Maid, 2:14).

MAMBRINO PATCHEN (brother to Lady Thorn, 2:18¼), by Mambrino Chief; dam by Gano, son of American Eclipse.

REDMON'S ABDALLAH PATCHEN, got by Alexander's Abdallah, son of Rysdyk's Hambletonian; dam Lady Valentine, by Redmon's Valentine, son of Imp. Valentine; 2d dam by Shakespeare; 3d dam by Potomac; 4th dam by Blackburn's Whip.

ALEXANDER'S ABDALLAH (sire of Goldsmith Maid, 2:14), got by Rysdyk's Hambletonian; dam Katy Darling, by Bay Roman.

SUNNYSIDE.

Light Bay Mare, foaled 1876. Bred by G. W. Swartz, Ala.

BY RICHELIEU (thoroughbred, who could pace and trot a 3:00 minute gait.)

In foal to Mambrino Patchen.

First dam Abdallah Belle, by Gum Elastic, by American Clay.

Second dam Lady Abdallah (dam of Granville, 2:26), by Alexander's Abdallah.

MAMBRINO PATCHEN (brother to Lady Thorn, 2:18¼), by Mambrino Chief; dam by Gano, son of American Eclipse

RICHELIEU (thoroughbred), got by Hiawatha; dam Fanny McAllister, by O'Meara; 2d dam by Imp. Leviathan.

GUM ELASTIC, got by American Clay; dam Laytham Lass, by Alexander's Abdallah; 2d dam by Mambrino Chief; 3d dam by Bellfounder.

ALEXANDER'S ABDALLAH (sire of Goldsmith Maid, 2:14), by Rysdyk's Hambletonian; dam Katy Darling, by Bay Roman.

No. 48.

MADALINE MAMBRINO.

Black Mare, foaled May, 1870.   Bred by L. Herr.
BY MAMBRINO PATCHEN.

In foal to Arnold.

First dam Arabian Belle, by Imp. Fysaul (Arabian.)
Second dam Sultana.
Third dam Old Sultana.

ARNOLD, got by Goldsmith's Abdallah, 2:30, son of Volunteer; dam
Sally Neal (dam of Hambrino Belle, 2:25½), by Mambrino
Chief.

MAMBRINO PATCHEN (brother to Lady Thorn, 2:18¼), by Mambrino
Chief; dam by Gano, son of American Eclipse; 2d dam by son
of Sir William, by Sir Archy.

No. 49.

GIRLIE GUNN.

Dark Grey Mare, foaled 1879.   Bred by Herr and Gunn.
BY MAMBRINO PATCHEN.

In foal to Arnold.

First dam by Lightning.
Second dam by Grey Eagle.
Third dam by Blackburn's Whip.

ARNOLD, got by Goldsmith's Abdallah, 2:30, son of Volunteer; dam
Sally Neal (dam of Hambrino Belle, 2:15½), by Mambrino
Chief.

MAMBRINO PATCHEN (brother to Lady Thorn, 2:18¼), by Mambrino
Chief; dam by Gano, son of American Eclipse; 2d dam by a son
of Sir William.

LIGHTNING, by Lexington, son of Boston.

GREY EAGLE, by Woodpecker, son of Bertrand.

BLACKBURN'S WHIP, by Imp. Whip.

PEARLY ROTHSCHILDS.

Gray Mare, foaled June, 1874. Bred by L. Herr.

BY ROTHSCHILDS.

In foal to Arnold.

First dam, Madaline Mambrino, by Mambrino Patchen.
Second dam, Arabian Belle, by Imp. Fysaul, Arabian.
Third dam, Sultana, Arabian.
Fourth dam, Old Sultana.

ARNOLD, by Goldsmith's Abdallah, 2:30 (son of Volunteer); dam, Sally
Neal (dam of Hambrino Belle, 2:25½), by Mambrino Chief.

ROTHSCHILDS, got by Mambrino Patchen; dam, by Alexander's Edwin Forrest; 2d dam, by Downing's Black Highlander; 3d dam, by
Lance, by American Eclipse.

MAMBRINO PATCHEN (brother to Lady Thorn, 2:18¼), by Mambrino
Chief; dam, by Gano, son of American Eclipse; 2d dam, by son of
Sir William, by Sir Archy.

MAGGIE MARSHALL.

Brown Mare. Bred in Mason County, Ky.

BY TELEGRAPH (Bradford's).

In foal to Mambrino Patchen.

First dam, by Prince Richard (thoroughbred).

MAMBRINO PATCHEN (brother to Lady Thorn, 2:18¼), by Mambrino Chief; dam, by Gano, son of American Eclipse; 2d dam, by
a son of Sir William, by Sir Archy.

TELEGRAPH, by Hill's Vermont Black Hawk, son of Sherman Morgan;
dam, by Vermont Hambletonian.

VERMONT HAMBLETONIAN, got by Harris' Hambletonian, son of
Bishop's Hambletonian; dam, by Comet.

KING'S BEAUTY.

Brown Filly, foaled 1878.   Bred by Herr & Downing.

BY MAMBRINO KING.

In foal to Arnold.
  First dam, by Glencoe, Jr., by Imp. Glencoe.
  Second dam, by Lexington, by Boston.
  Third dam, by Ruffian.
  Fourth dam, by Leviathan.
  Fifth dam, by Stockholder.
  Sixth dam, by Pacolet.
  Seventh dam, by Imp. Citizen.

ARNOLD, got by Goldsmith's Abdallah 2:30 (son of Volunteer); dam, Sallie Neale (the dam of Hambrino Belle, 2:25½), by Mambrino Chief.

MAMBRINO KING, got by Mambrino Patchen; dam, by Alexander's Edwin Forrest; 2d dam (the dam of Fisk's Mambrino Chief, 2:29½), by Birmingham; 3d dam, by Bertrand; 4th dam, by Sumpter; 5th dam, by Imp. Buzzard.

LYDIA ANN.

Chestnut Mare, foaled 1868.   Bred by John S. Whaley, Harrison County, Ky.

BY INDIAN CHIEF.

In foal to Mambrino Patchen.
  First dam, by Redmon's Valentine, son of Imp. Valentine.

MAMBRINO PATCHEN (full brother to Lady Thorn, 2:18¼), by Mambrino Chief; dam, by Gano, son of American Eclipse; 2d dam, by son of Sir William, by Sir Archy.

INDIAN CHIEF (sire of Warrior, 2:26), got by Blood's Black Hawk, son of Vermont Black Hawk; dam, Lou Berry, by Ned Forrest, son of Young Bashaw; 2d dam, Fan, by Tucker's Grey Messenger.

REDMON'S VALENTINE, by Imp. Valentine.

No. 54.

KING GIRL.

Chestnut Mare, foaled 1878. Bred by R. S. Strader.

BY MAMBRINO KING.

In foal to Arnold.

First dam, Leah (trial, 2:26), by Wilson's Blue Bull.
Second dam, by Tom Hal (pacer).

ARNOLD, got by Goldsmith's Abdallah, 2:30 (son of Volunteer); dam,
Sally Neal (dam of Hambrino Belle, 2:25½), by Mambrino Chief,
&c.

MAMBRINO KING, got by Mambrino Patchen; dam, by Alexander's Edwin Forrest; 2d dam (the dam of Fisk's Mambrino Chief, 2:29½),
by Birmingham; 3d dam, by Bertrand; 4th dam, by Sumpter; 5th
dam by Imp. Buzzard.

BLUE BULL (Wilson's), got by Pruden's Blue Bull; dam, not traced.

No. 55.

FRANKIE LYONS.

Sorrel Mare, foaled 1880. Bred by Herr & Lyons.

BY MAMBRINO PATCHEN.

In foal to Arnold.

First dam, by Hughes' Edwin Forrest (by Alexander's Edwin Forrest).
Second dam, by Bald Hornet (pacer).

ARNOLD, got by Goldsmith's Abdallah, 2:30 (son of Volunteer); dam,
Sally Neal (dam of Hambrino Belle, 2:25½), by Mambrino Chief;
2d dam, by Terror; 3d dam, by Doublehead; 4th dam, by American
Eclipse.

MAMBRINO PATCHEN (full brother to Lady Thorn, 2:18¼), by Mambrino Chief; dam, by Gano, son of American Eclipse; 2d dam, by
a son of Sir William, by Sir Archy.

HUGHES' EDWIN FORREST, by Alexander's Edwin Forrest.

VERSAILLES MAID.

Bay Mare.   Bred by Jesse H. Farra.

BY HURST & THORNTON'S ABDALLAH (son of Alexander's Abdallah).

In foal to Arnold.

First dam, by Paddy Burns, by Grey Eagle.

ARNOLD, by Goldsmith's Abdallah, 2:30 (son of Volunteer); dam, Sally Neal (dam of Hambrino Belle, 2:25½), by Mambrino Chief.

HURST & THORNTON'S ABDALLAH, by Alexander's Abdallah (sire of Goldsmith Maid, 2:14), son of Rysdyk's Hambletonian; dam, by old St. Lawrence.

PADDY BURNS, by Grey Eagle, &c.

TRANBIANA.

Bay Mare, foaled 1871.   Bred by a Mr. Harris, of Woodford County, Ky.

BY MAMBRINO TRANBY.

First dam, by Iron Duke, by C. M. Clay.
Second dam, by Todhunter's Sir Wallace.
Third dam, by a son of Blackburn's Whip.

MAMBRINO TRANBY, got by Mambrino Patchen; dam, by Mahomet, son of Imp. Sovereign; 2d dam, by Imp. Tranby; 3d dam, by Aratus; 4th dam, by Josephus; 5th dam, by Columbus, &c.

IRON DUKE, got by Cassius M. Clay; dam, by Young Cleveland; 2d dam, by Bishop's Hambletonian; 3d dam, by Commander, son of Imp. Messenger.

FANNY HASERACK.

Brown Bay Mare, foaled ——.   Bred by J. M. Shreve.

BY WASHINGTON DENMARK.

In foal to Mambrino Patchen.

First dam by Haserack, a Copperbottom horse.

MAMBRINO PATCHEN (brother to Lady Thorn, 2:18¼), by Mambrino
   Chief; dam by Gano, son of American Eclipse; 2d dam by son
   of Sir William.

MOLLIE LINTHICUM.

Brown Mare, foaled 1872.   Bred by C. G. Linthicum.

BY A SON OF RED EYE, by Boston.

In foal to Arnold.

First dam by son of old St. Lawrence, trotter.

ARNOLD, by Goldsmith's Abdallah, 2:30, son of Volunteer; dam Sally
   Neal (dam of Hambrino Belle, 2:25½), by Mambrino Chief; 2d
   dam by Terror; 3d dam by Doublehead; 4th dam by American
   Eclipse.

MOLLY.

Grey Mare, an extra saddle mare and breeder.

BY BALD STOCKINGS.

Dam's pedigree unknown.

BALD STOCKINGS, pacer, by Tom Hal, pacer; dam by Chinn's Copperbottom; 2d dam by Tarquin.

BASHAW BELLE.

Grey Mare; foaled 1869. Bred by George W. Greever, Leavenworth, Kansas.

BY GREEN'S BASHAW.

In foal to King Rene.

First dam, Gray Mary, by St. Louis.
Second dam, by Clay Trustee.
Third dam, by Tom Watson.
Fourth dam, Mirth, by Medoc.
Fifth dam, Lucy Alexander, by Buford's Alexander.
Sixth dam, by Haxall's Moses.
Seventh dam, by Duke of Bedford.
Eighth dam, by Old Union.
Ninth dam, by Imp. Dabster.

KING RENE (sire of Fugue, 2·27½). got by Belmont (sire of Nutwood, 2:18¾); dam, Blandina, by Mambrino Chief (sire of Lady Thorn, 2:18¼), &c.

GREEN'S BASHAW (sire of Josephus, 2:19¾; Hambletonian Bashaw, 2:21¼; Rose of Washington, 2:21¾, &c.), got by Vernol's Black Hawk (son of of Long Island Black Hawk); dam, Belle, by Webber's Tom Thumb; 2d dam, the Charles Kent mare (dam of Rysdyk's Hambletonian), by Imp. Bellfounder, &c.

GRAY MARE.

Foaled 1879. Bred by Jas. A. Grinstead, Lexington, Ky.

BY ADMINISTRATOR, 2:29½.

In foal to Hambrino, 2:21¼.

First dam, Bashaw Belle, by Green's Bashaw.
Second dam, Grey Mary, by St. Louis.

Third dam, by Clay Trustee.
Fourth dam, by Tom Watson.
Fifth dam, Mirth, by Medoc.
Sixth dam, Lucy Alexander, by Buford's Alexander.
Seventh dam, by Haxal's Moses.
Eighth dam, by Duke of Bedford.
Ninth dam, by Old Union.
Tenth dam, by Imp. Dabster.

HAMBRINO (sire of Hambrino Belle, 2:25½), got by Edward Everett (sire of Judge Fullerton, 2:18, &c.); dam, Mambrina, by Mambrino Chief (sire of Lady Thorn, 2:18¼, &c.); 2d dam, Susie, by Imp. Margrave, &c.

ADMINISTRATOR, 2:29½ (sire of Catchfly, 2:19; Executor, 2:26, &c.); got by Rysdyk's Hambletonian; dam, by Mambrino Chief; 2d dam, by Arabian Tartar, &c.

GREEN'S BASHAW (sire of Josephus, 2:19¾; Hambletonian Bashaw, 2:21¼; Rose of Washington, 2:21¾, &c.), got by Vernol's Black Hawk (son of Long Island Black Hawk); dam, Belle, by Webber's Tom Thumb; 2d dam, the Charles Kent mare (dam of Rysdyk's Hambletonian), by Imp. Bellfounder, &c.

No. 63.

BAY MARE.

Foaled 1875. Bred by James A. Grinstead, Lexington. Ky.

BY GILROY (by Lexington).

First dam, Kitty Forrest, by Alexander's Edwin Forrest.
Second dam, Kitty Kirkman, by Fanning's Canada Chief.
Third dam, by Fanning's Tobe.
Fourth dam, by Imp. Leviathan.

EDWIN FORREST (Alexander's), sire of Billy Hoskins, 2:26¼, and Champaign, 2.30, got by Bay Kentucky Hunter; dam, by Watkins' Young Highlander.

GELDINGS.

—o—

No. 64.

RED BOY.

Bay Gelding, foaled 1878, Bred by Herr and Garth.

BY MAMBRINO PATCHEN.

First dam by Henderson's Davy Crockett, son of old Davy Crockett, fast pacer.

Second dam by Tom Hal, pacer.

MAMBRINO PATCHEN (brother to Lady Thorn, 2:18¼), by Mambrino Chief; dam by Gano, son of American Eclipse ; 2d dam by a son of Sir William, by Sir Archy.

No. 65.

BLACK BOY.

Black Gelding, foaled 1880. Bred by Jno. Stout.

BY MAMBRINO ABDALLAH.

First dam Sally Southworth (full sister to Lady Stout, 2:29, at three years old), by Mambrino Patchen.

Second dam Puss Prall, by Mark Time.

Third dam by Daniel Webster.

MAMBRINO ABDALLAH. got by Mambrino Patchen; dam Lady Ayres' by Redmon's Abdallah Patchen, son of Alexander's Abdallah; 2d dam Lady Abdallah (dam of Granville, 2:26), by Alexander's Abdallah.

MAMBRINO PATCHEN (brother to Lady Thorn, 2:18¼), by Mambrino

Chief; dam by Gano, son of American Eclipse; 2d dam by a son of Sir William, by Sir Archy.

MARK TIME, got by Berthune; dam by Paddy Carey, son of Friendship, by Pantaloon; 2d dam Jenny Gray, by Robin Gray.

DANIEL WEBSTER, got by Lance, by American Eclipse; dam by Nall's Diomed; 2d dam by Blackburn's Buzzard; 3d dam by Imp. Medley.

No. 66.

COUNTRY BOY.

Sorrel Gelding, foaled 1878.   Bred by Herr & Jacoby.

BY MAMBRINO PATCHEN.

First dam, Country Girl, by Country Gentleman.

Second dam, by Canadian Chief (and is the dam of Joe Hooker, sire of Maud Macy, 2:27¾ and Bushwhacker, 2:29½).

Third dam, by Kavanaugh, son of Bertrand.

Fourth dam, by American Eclipse.

Fifth dam, by Potomac.

MAMBRINO PATCHEN (full brother to Lady Thorn, 2:18¼), by Mambrino Chief; dam, by Gano, son of American Eclipse; 2d dam, by a son of Sir William, by Sir Archy, &c.

COUNTRY GENTLEMAN, by Rysdyk's Hambletonian; dam, by Highlander, by Imp. Highlander; 2d dam, by Cogswell's Consul, by Bean's Consul; 3d dam, by Duroc.

CANADIAN CHIEF, by Blackburn's Davy Crockett; dam, by Blackburn's Whip.

Numbers 63 and 64 make a coach team 16 hands high.

No. 67.

SORREL GELDING.

Foaled 1879.

BY HAILSTORM (son of Mambrino Patchen).

Numbers 63 and 64 make coach team 16 hands high.

DOCTOR L. HERR'S

CELEBRATED BLISTERING FLUID.

PRICE, $1.00 PER BOTTLE.

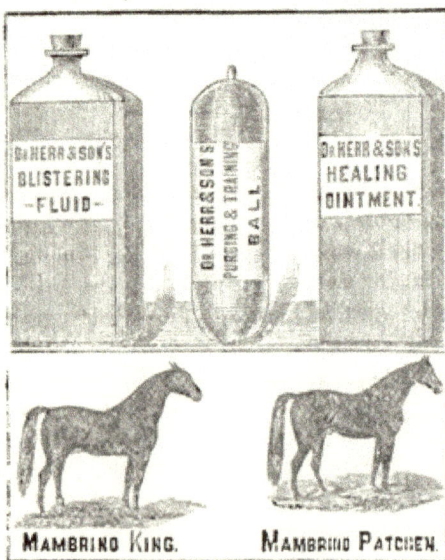

MAMBRINO KING.   MAMBRINO PATCHEN.

Which has stood the practical test for over 35 years in his extensive practice, and has effected more cures and given greater relief to suffering animals, and saved more money to owners in the successful treatment of valuable animals than any medicine that ever came under his extensive experience, and answering for a greater number of diseases, and safer than any other active blistering application, never leaving a blemish, and not necessary to tie up a horse's head to prevent him from biting the blistered surface, and to which his many old patrons can testify, and which are numerous in Kentucky. When a medicine is put before the public as an infallible remedy for all diseases, external and internal, and for diseases so opposite and different in character, the person so recommending either does not know or is trying to humbug the people.

DR. HERR & SON'S BLISTERING FLUID

Is not recommended to the public by guess or for deception, neither will it be embellished with fancy wrappers or counterfeit show, but for its tried and known value, having stood the test in active practice for years. It is used as

an external application, but in no way interfering with internal or constitu-
tional treatment, but in many cases of great service as an auxiliary to their
action and effects, by the counter irritation produced by the Blistering Fluid,
and in patients that are languid or debilitated, the Blistering Fluid becoming
absorbed to some extent into the circulation, acts as a tonic and invigorator
of the system, and having also through the circulation a mild diuretic effect
upon the kidneys, which in many cases is so desirable—such as Pneumonia,
Pleurisy, Dropsy, Influenza, Farcy, &c.   The Blistering Fluid is recommended for the following named complaints : For all Glandular and Throat
Affections, Distemper, etc.; for all Callous and Bony Enlargements. Splint,
Spavin, Curb, Bucked Shins, in running and trotting horses, for Shoulder
Strains, for deep-seated and Chronic Lameness, for Contraction or Shrinkage
of Muscles in Shoulders or Hips (ordinarily called Sweenie), for Counter
Irritation on side of jaw, for Sore Eyes; for anointing Rowels and Seaton
Strings, to induce a free and copious discharge.   For all Tumors (muscular)
the Blistering Fluid will reduce them by absorption, or if too far advanced,
with a tendency to form abscess (puss or matter), it will speedily draw it to
the surface, ready for the lance.   Fistula and Poll-evil, on their first appear-
ance, before matter forms, will often yield to its application every fifteen days
to twenty days.   For counter irritation in violent cases of Colic or Inflam-
mation of the Bowels, rubbing it under the belly and flanks, &c.   Nothing
will forward or increase the growth of horn or hoof more rapidly, and grow
off quarter cracks and false quarters than the Blistering Fluid, by rubbing it
an inch high above the hoofs every twenty days, which stimulates the coro-
nets to increased action in the secretion of new and healthy horn or hoof.
In dropsical effusion under the belly (commonly called Farcy), by rubbing
the enlarged parts once a week with the Blistering Fluid it will stimulate the
parts to healthy action by causing absorption of the fluid or serum between
the muscles of the abdomen and skin, and also through the channel of the
kidneys, by its diuretic effect by absorption into the circulation.   For erup-
tions or scaly points, and surfeit of the skin or muscles, nothing restores
healthy action more speedily or effectually, and so easily applied.   For
all itchiness of the skin it will allay in one application.   One bottle will
often save a horse worth not only hundreds, but thousands of dollars.   The
Blistering Fluid is rubbed in with the hand, using a good deal of friction, and
applied slow and well rubbed in, and as much or little is used, the effect will
be more or less active, corresponding with the amount rubbed in.   In the
winter, when the coat or hair is long, the parts to be blistered may be clipped,
or for a quick effect can be shaved.   In the summer, after shedding, when
the coat is thin and short, it can be applied to the natural coat or skin.   For
the above named diseases, it can be applied once in from seven to twenty
days. In chronic cases, every twenty days.   For Fistula and Poll-evil, every
twenty days.   After applying, it is not to be interrupted by oiling or bath-
ing ; not to be interfered with until the gummy scurf dries, and will rub off

with the hand or brush, after which, if necessary, the Blistering Fluid can be renewed.

HORSE SURGERY

Practiced as heretofore. Trotting stock constantly for sale, from weanling to aged horses, for track and road use. Orders filled for all descriptions of horses.

MANY STRONG CERTIFICATES

Could be given from the best horse and stock men in Kentucky ; but being tiresome to read, and to save space, I will give the names of only a few who are reliable and well known, and who have indorsed their names, and who know the value of the Blistering Fluid, from actual test upon their own stock and others, whose stock have been so successfully treated by Dr. Herr's remedies and practice, and who can be written to by parties from a distance for their opinions, and whose names are given below.

BY ORDER

These medicines can be sent by mail or express to any part of the country. Persons wishing agencies to sell on commission can be furnished by application to Dr. L. Herr & Sons, or to H. H. Barnes & Co., druggists, Lexington, Ky., general depots for supplies, and who will forward according to orders.

WE, THE UNDERSIGNED,

Fully endorse the value and curative properties of Dr. Herr's above described Blistering Fluid and Purging Balls :

HON. JAMES B. BECK, United States Senator, Kentucky.
HON. J. C. S. BLACKBURN, Member of Congress.
GEN. WM. PRESTON, Lexington, Ky.
M. H. SANFORD, Preakness Stud Farm, Lexington, Ky.
JAS. A. GRINSTEAD, Walnut Hill.
GEN. A. BUFORD, Bosque Bonita Stud Farm.
GEN. J. F. ROBINSON, President Lexington Association.
MAJOR H. C. McDOWELL.
MAJOR B. G. THOMAS, Dixiana.
MAJOR JOHN R. VILEY, Lexington, Ky.
LESLIE COMBS, JR, Spring Station, Ky.
HON. T. J. MEGIBBEN, Fairview.
JAS. H. McCREARY, Kentucky.

H. P. McGrath, McGrathiana Stud Farm.
Daniel Swigert, Spring Station, Ky.
John M. Clay, Ashland, Ky.
Col. S. D. Bruce, Turf, Field and Farm.
A. Keene Richards, Blue Grass Stud Farm, Ky.
Col. Richard West, Edge Hill, Ky
Hon. Zeb Ward, Kentucky.
A. G. Peters, Kentucky.
James Miller.
Col. R. G. Stoner.
Col. R. S. Strader, Lexington, Ky.
Treacy & Wilson.
Logan Railey, Versailles, Ky.

None genuine without having Dr. Herr's name blown on the bottle.   Price, $1 per bottle.

.

www.ingramcontent.com/pod-product-compliance
Lightning Source LLC
Chambersburg PA
CBHW032116080426
42733CB00008B/959

* 9 7 8 3 3 3 7 2 2 6 2 6 8 *